386. 4

re

Series 601

*From the opening of the Bridgewater Canal
in 1761, until well into the 19th Century,
the canal system in Great Britain grew at
a tremendous pace. At its height, there were
over 6,000 miles of navigable rivers and canals
covering the length and breadth of the country,
supplying the vital link between mines, farms,
factories and ports.*

*The story of how this was achieved, of the
colourful characters who dug the canals and
operated them, is here depicted in words and
pictures, in all its fascinating detail.*

INDEX

The story of our
CANALS

by CAROLYN HUTCHINGS

with illustrations by
ROGER HALL

Ladybird Books Loughborough

Introduction

Early in the 18th century, Britain was largely agricultural, but workers were beginning to move away from the land to the new textile and iron-smelting industries. Steam was replacing wind and water as a source of power and coal was therefore needed in large quantities. The new industries wanted more and more materials to make their products and urgently needed better communications for distributing the manufactured goods. Coal could be delivered to the factories only in small quantities by wagon or by pack-horse, because the roads were not suited to heavy traffic. In wet and wintry weather they were often impassable.

Rivers had always been used for transport and efforts were made to improve them. They were widened, deepened, or straightened—a process called 'canalisation'. The rivers Weaver and Trent were made navigable and the Mersey and the Irwell made usable to Manchester.

By the middle of the 18th century, Manchester was growing in importance as an industrial centre and it is not surprising that the first canal was cut in Lancashire. Plans were made to canalise the Sankey Brook, a stream which passed from the St. Helens coal mines to the Mersey. The project proved impracticable and instead, the wholly artificial St. Helens Canal was dug. The setting up of our vast canal system was started and the success of the St. Helens Canal showed that man-made waterways could be cut almost anywhere in the land.

The first English canal

The Bridgewater was the first canal project planned from the start to be a completely man-made inland waterway. Francis Egerton, Duke of Bridgewater, had to solve the problem of moving coal in large quantities from his mines at Worsley in Lancashire to Manchester, eight miles away, where it was urgently needed. The Duke had toured France, Holland and Italy and had seen the use made of waterways on the continent.

He chose as his engineer the millwright James Brindley, who with the help of John Gilbert, the Duke's agent, surveyed the canal line. The route planned, which was to be all on one level, entailed crossing the River Irwell and Brindley proposed building an aqueduct to carry the canal thirty-eight feet above the river. The idea was ridiculed by many people but the Duke had great faith in Brindley's ability and the Barton Aqueduct was successfully built and opened in 1761.

Brindley took the waterway right to the very coal face in the Worsley mines so that coal could be dug and loaded directly into small boats, forty-seven feet long and four and a half feet wide. These were towed in 'trains' along the underground canals. The remarkable underground system included forty-six miles of canal, locks and an inclined plane where boats were hauled up a slope.

The Bridgewater Canal was so successful that following its opening the price of coal in Manchester was halved.

The canal was later extended to Runcorn, where it joined the River Mersey and provided a better communication between Manchester and Liverpool. This resulted in the charge for carrying goods between the two towns being reduced from five shillings per ton to two shillings and sixpence per ton.

Canal mania

Even before the first canal, the Bridgewater, was finished, industrialists and colliery owners had realised the practical value of water transport, and an era of canal building began. During the fifty to sixty years following the opening of the Bridgewater Canal in 1761, the Mersey, Trent, Severn and Thames rivers were linked by narrow canals. There were broader waterways in some parts of the country, too.

Enthusiasm for the new canals came from the people who hoped to benefit from them. These were mine owners, like the Duke of Bridgewater, who wanted to increase their profits, and manufacturers like Josiah Wedgwood the potter, who hoped, with an improved transport system, that the market for his products would develop. Before the advent of the canal system, Wedgwood had to ship china clay from Devon and Cornwall to Liverpool, up the River Weaver to Winsford and then by pack-horse to his potteries near Stoke-on-Trent, a long and expensive journey.

Some canals, like the Ellesmere Canal, were projected for the easy transport of agricultural produce and occasionally merchants hoped that the trade of small ports could be increased by building canals into the hinterland as in the case of the Chester Canal.

The most common arguments in favour of canals, however, were that raw materials could be brought more cheaply to the factories and finished products could more easily be carried away.

The Act and the money

Before the work of building a canal could begin, two major arrangements had to be made. Money for the project had to be raised and the permission of Parliament had to be obtained.

The promoters of the canal would first place an advertisement in the local newspaper, stating the advantages of the proposed navigation and asking all those interested to attend a meeting. These meetings were often held in the Assembly Room of an inn.

At this meeting, a committee would be formed, a subscription list opened and an engineer appointed. He would survey and report upon a route and prepare an estimate of the cost of the task.

Parliament, if it approved of the project, would pass an Act, stating details of the proposed route and giving the canal company rights to buy land and obtain water. The Act also protected the interests of those who might lose by the construction of the canal. There was always opposition and this is one of the reasons why an Act was necessary. Landowners affected were compensated and so were millers and factory owners who feared a loss of water.

Since canals were local projects, the money was usually raised locally from those who stood to gain from the scheme. These were colliery and works owners, merchants and tradesmen. A good deal of money also came from noblemen, landed gentry and the clergy. Those interested bought shares, which were usually sold in units of £100.

The engineers

When canals were built in the eighteenth and nine-teenth centuries, there were no trained engineers as we know them today and, at first, no trained labourers. It was fortunate for the Duke of Bridgewater that his engineer, James Brindley, was a man of great inventive ability. Brindley had had little education and could scarcely read or write. So successful was the Bridgewater Canal that Brindley was invited to work on many other ambitious schemes. It is likely that he died of overwork. He did not even have the help of reliable maps. The first Ordnance Survey Maps did not appear until 1801.

There were many other fine canal engineers, such as John Smeaton, Thomas Telford, William Jessop, John Rennie and Benjamin Outram.

Thomas Telford built the Chirk and Pontcysyllte Aqueducts on the Llangollen Canal. Canal building however, formed only a part of his work. He also built the Menai Suspension Bridge, parts of London Docks, bridges, roads, canal warehouses and churches.

John Rennie was known for his wider canals, the Kennet and Avon, the Lancaster and the Rochdale. Like Telford, he built fine stone aqueducts. William Jessop, consulted about many canals, was also an iron-master and a builder of horse railways. Benjamin Outram, famous for the Peak Forest Canal, also built tramways. John Smeaton made his name, not only because of his canal projects but as a builder of har-bours, bridges, and the Eddystone Lighthouse.

Thomas Telford and the Pontcysyllte Aqueduct.

How the canals were built

Most canals were cut before the invention of any mechanical tools. Tens of thousands of 'navvies' or 'cutters' dug the channels from one end of the country to the other, using only spades, picks and barrows and helped by horses. The canals were constructed with sloping sides and flat bottoms. Then, to prevent water escaping, they were lined with puddled clay, which is clay worked with so much water that it forms a watertight seal.

As far as possible, the early canals followed the contours, since it was easier and cheaper to take a canal round a hill rather than through, or over it. However, as speed became more important, canals were cut straighter, with long flights of locks, aqueducts and tunnels. The method for tunnels was to cut into the hillside from each end. At intervals along the line of the tunnel, shafts were sunk down to the level of the canal and men would dig in both directions, often working by candlelight. The spoil would be drawn back up through the shaft. The shafts were left to ventilate the tunnels. Miners, with their expert knowledge, were engaged to reinforce tunnel cutting gangs.

The construction gangs were rough men and village people were afraid of them. They built themselves crude huts from whatever materials were available, moving from site to site as work progressed across the countryside.

Locks

A boat can be raised from one level to another by means of a lock. This consists of a chamber, usually built of brick or masonry with a heavy timber gate, or gates, at each end. The gates close in a 'V' shape and water pressing against them keeps them shut. They are opened by pushing against balance beams, which are strong timbers fitted along the top edge of the gate.

In the lock wall, and sometimes in the gate too, there are paddles which can be opened to allow water to pass through sluices into the lock, or out of it. Paddles can be raised or lowered by turning gear wheels with a cranked handle, called a windlass.*

Stop locks, with 'guillotine' or 'portcullis gates' were sometimes put in where two canals joined, to prevent one canal company poaching water from another.

The longest 'flight' in the United Kingdom is at Tardebigge, on the Worcester and Birmingham Canal, where there are thirty locks, one after the other.

At Foxton, on the Grand Union Canal, there is a flight of locks without a stretch of water, or pound, between each chamber. Locks which pass straight from one chamber into the next, and where the top gates of one lock are the bottom gates of the next are called 'staircase' or 'risers'.

At Beeston, on the Shropshire Union Canal, the lock is built of cast-iron plates bolted together. They were used because the ground below was not firm but consisted of running sand.

* For detailed diagram, see front endpaper.

Lifts and inclined planes

The engineers found other ways of moving boats up and down hills, ways which were quicker, less expensive than locks, and less extravagant in the use of water.

Higher and lower canal levels might be connected by steeply sloping railways. On the Bude Canal in Cornwall, there were six of these inclined planes and the tub boats used were fitted with four iron wheels which ran up and down the rails on the incline. At Foxton, on the Grand Union Canal, colossal tanks called caissons, capable of holding a pair of narrow boats, were pulled sideways, up and down, by wire ropes, powered by steam winding gear. At the lower end, the caissons were immersed in the canal basin, to allow boats to enter or leave through lift-up gates set in the ends of the tanks. The incline took twelve minutes to raise or lower boats, compared with over an hour by way of existing, narrow staircase locks. The expected additional traffic did not materialise and the incline was used only for about ten years.

There were also vertical lifts with two caissons suspended by wires from wheels. Water was added to the uppermost tank so that, when it began to descend, its weight raised the lower tank.

But the planes and lifts have now all ceased to operate, except for the immense Anderton Lift in Cheshire, which transfers boats between the Trent and Mersey Canal and the River Weaver. It is electrically operated and can raise or lower boats over fifty feet in five minutes.

Foxton Incline.

Canal tunnels

Several canal tunnels are less than one hundred yards long but the longest, the Standedge, on the Huddersfield Narrow Canal, is over three miles long. The first main line canal tunnel in England was the Harecastle on the Trent and Mersey Canal. It was 2,897 yards long and took eleven years to dig out. It was only nine feet wide and did not have a tow-path. Its narrowness caused such delays that a second tunnel was built alongside. Both tunnels were used for ninety years, one for northbound boats and the other for southbound traffic.

It was cheaper to build a narrow tunnel with no tow-path.

In the days of horse-drawn boats, the children or the women would lead the horse over the hill while the boat was 'legged' or 'shafted' through the tunnel. 'Legging', an exhausting task, was performed by two men, who lay on their backs, one each side at the fore end of the boat, and pushed against the tunnel walls with their feet. If the tunnel was wide and they could not reach the side walls, 'legging' boards or wings which projected over the side of the boat, were fitted, again at the fore end, and the men lay on these.

In low tunnels one man could 'leg' an empty boat by lying on the cabin top and pressing against the roof with his feet. 'Shafting' involved pushing with a long pole against the top or sides of the tunnel, while walking from forward to aft along the length of the boat.

Chains were fastened along the walls of some tunnels so that boatmen could pull themselves through.

Bridges

The various canal companies developed their own style of bridge design. The most common pattern is the single brick arch, with a towing path beneath it. The canal usually narrowed beneath the bridge and was built this way for reasons of economy. This narrowing is referred to as the bridge 'hole'. The bridges were built to carry roads or paths over the canal, while some were 'accommodation' bridges. These reconnected land-owner's fields which had been divided when the water-way was first cut.

There were roving, or turnover bridges which carried the tow-path from one side of the canal to the other. A towing horse could use a bridge like this without being unhitched from the boat.

A split, or divided bridge, comprised timber decking on iron brackets projecting half across the canal from each side, but not quite meeting in the middle. When a horse-drawn boat approached the bridge, the horse was slowed up and the tow-line dropped through the slit between the two parts of the bridge.

Along the Llangollen and Oxford Canals, there are lift-up bridges. The weight of the bridge is balanced by heavy beams, making it easy to raise by pulling on the chain provided. On the Peak Forest Canal there are opening bridges, which turn aside.

The continuous wear of tow-lines cut deep into the brickwork of many bridges. Protective iron bands were fixed to the underside of the bridge, but even these were deeply scored by rope wear.

Aqueducts

Aqueducts were built to carry canals over river valleys, streams, roadways, or other canals. The first aqueduct was built by Brindley, to carry the Bridgewater Canal over the River Irwell at Barton. It was a masonry aqueduct, lined with clay.

Brindley's plan for an aqueduct was considered an ambitious and ridiculous venture, but its success inspired other engineers and in South Wales, for example, on the Brecon and Abergavenny Canal, there are six aqueducts in the space of twelve miles.

The weight and expense of bricks meant that it was impracticable to build very large masonry aqueducts. Telford experimented with the use of cast-iron. In 1795 work began on the magnificent Pontcysyllte Aqueduct, which carries the Llangollen Canal more than one hundred and twenty feet above the River Dee. The cast-iron trough is over one thousand feet long. It is supported by eighteen masonry piers, which were built partly hollow, to save expense. There is a tow-path on the down-stream side but, on the up-stream side, there is a sheer drop to the river below. The aqueduct took eight years to build.

At the end of the 19th century, Brindley's Barton Aqueduct was replaced by a steel swing aqueduct. It was built to span the Manchester Ship Canal and revolves on a central pier. A system of gates at the end of the trough and at adjoining ends of the Bridgewater Canal ensure that the tank is always kept full of water.

Water supply

The Acts of Parliament which authorised the building of canals, also gave the canal companies power to take water from streams, rivers and other sources to feed the canal. Even so, one of the biggest problems facing the canal engineer was to get water into the canal, and keep it there. Each time a boat passed through a lock, a lockful of water was lost from the summit, the highest part of the canal. The average narrow lock needs 25,000 gallons each time it is used and a broad lock needs 60,000 gallons.

Reservoirs were built to maintain adequate supplies of water at the summit. Water from the reservoirs flowed into the canal along narrow channels, or feeders. Occasionally, the summit level of the canal was deepened, to act as a reservoir itself. Some canal engineers installed large beam engines to pump water back up the canal from a lower level.

Efforts were made to save water at the locks. Side ponds were dug alongside, which meant that roughly half the water from an emptying lock could be diverted into the side pond to be used to partially fill the lock when it was next needed. Boatmen were instructed to move alternately up and down locks to avoid wastage. Sometimes locks were padlocked at night and on Sundays.

As the number of boats increased, the problem of water shortage grew. In dry summers, because of lack of water, boats could only be partly loaded. With a lighter load they needed less water in the canal to keep them afloat.

During wet weather there was sometimes too much water and it had to be run off to avoid flooding.

How boats were propelled

It was sometimes possible to sail barges on river navigations, or to allow them to drift downstream, controlled by long oars. Most canal boats however, were towed, sometimes by gangs of men, called bow-hauliers, sometimes by mules or pairs of donkeys, but generally by horses. Probably one horse could do the work of six men. A loaded narrow boat, hauled by one horse, moved at about two miles per hour and, when empty, at about three miles per hour. Two loaded boats, towed by one horse, travelled at only one and a half miles per hour and, when empty, at about two and a half miles per hour.

There were some strict overtaking rules. When boats met, travelling in opposite directions, one of the boatmen had to give way, stop his horse and drop his towline to let the other horse pass. It was generally understood that loaded boats were given right of way over unloaded craft.

However, horses needed food and rest, and many horse-drawn boats were replaced by craft equipped with steam-driven engines. These 'steamers' were not very successful since the engine and boiler took up much valuable cargo space and required constant attention to keep up the head of steam. Eventually the steam engine was replaced by a diesel unit, which took up less space and would run for many years without much trouble.

Tolls and goods carried

Canal companies obtained their revenue from tolls charged to boat owners. These tolls were set out in the Company's Act and could not be altered without further Parliamentary permission. The toll was calculated at the rate of a few pence, or parts of a penny, per ton per mile. Milestones were set up along the towpath to assist with the calculation of the distance carried.

When a boat was built, markings were cut into the wooden hull showing the draught of the boat when empty and when filled with various cargoes. Early in the 19th century however, a new method was adopted, depending on the freeboard – the depth of hull showing above the water. The freeboard was noted when the boat was empty and when loaded, and the figures were recorded in registers. The toll-clerk could then measure the freeboard with a gauging stick, check the figure with the register and charge the appropriate toll.

A few canal companies possessed weighing machines. The boat was floated over a cradle in a dock and the water drained off, leaving the boat ready for weighing.

The goods carried included chemicals, metals, building materials, manure, peat, coal, coke and charcoal, animals, and animal foods, foodstuffs and footwear. In wartime, soldiers and their weapons were carried. The least tolls were demanded for bulk cargoes like coal, and the most for finished goods, groceries and general merchandise.

The narrow boat

Canal working boats, known as 'Long' or 'Narrow' boats were generally about seventy feet long and seven feet wide and were designed to fit the locks on Brindley's Grand Trunk Canal. The first narrow boats were built entirely of wood with elm bottom and oak sides. To preserve the oak it was treated with chalico, a mixture of horse manure, cow hair and tar. The elm needed no treatment. Continual soaking in canal water kept the timber in good condition. Later boats were constructed with steel sides and elm bottom and were eventually built entirely of steel.

Narrow boats usually worked in pairs, one boat towing another, the towed boat being called the 'butty'. 'Butty' is an old English word meaning mate. A cabined boat was called a 'monkey' boat, named after Thomas Monk, born in Tipton, who was the first person to fit out a canal boat with cabin accommodation. For the larger boat families, a small sleeping cabin was also provided at the fore end of the butty.

A boatman who owned his boat was called a 'Number One'. Other boats belonged to carrying companies.

The boats could hold up to twenty-five tons.

To protect the cargo in bad weather, or from a possible wetting when the boat was rising in a lock, tarpaulins were strapped over a top plank which ran the length of the hold. When the canvasses were in place, the boat was said to be 'sheeted up'.

Other canal boats

Canal builders had made little attempt at standard-isation and the seventy foot narrow boat was not suitable for all canals. A fifty-eight foot long boat was designed, for example, to pass the short locks of some Yorkshire canals. Boats up to fourteen feet wide could operate the wide waterways, such as the Leeds and Liverpool Canal.

The compartment boats of Yorkshire attract much interest. Known as 'Tom Puddings' they carry coal, generally to Goole, where they are lifted out of the water by coal hoists and their contents tipped into coal-carrying, sea-going ships. A single tug will pull a train of up to thirty two-compartment boats each carrying thirty-five tons of coal.

Before the railways were built, most canals had a regular passenger-carrying service. The craft used were called 'packet boats'. The packet journey between Edinburgh and Glasgow, along the Forth and Clyde Canal took eleven hours, and dinner, bed and breakfast were provided.

'Fly boats' were express craft, carrying a maximum of twenty tons, and stopping only to change their tired horses. They had priority of passage over other craft and some were fitted with an S shaped blade at the fore end, which could cut through the towing ropes of boats which did not give way to them.

Ice breakers were used to keep the canal clear in winter. A gang of men held on to a rail running along the length of the boat and rocked the boat from side to side as it was pulled through the ice by several horses.

Railway competition

In colliery districts it was often impracticable to extend the canal to the coalface and instead, a tramway would be built. At first the tram rails were of brittle cast-iron and had to be replaced frequently but, by 1820, improved rails of wrought-iron were being used. In the early years of the nineteenth century, the steam locomotive engine was introduced. The Stockton and Darlington Railway was opened in 1825, and the success of Stephenson's locomotive 'Rocket' established a rail mania. People began to think that canals were old fashioned compared with the railways.

Transport by rail was a great deal faster than by water. Efforts were made to speed up canal transport. Instead of following contours, there was some straightening of canals to lessen distances. The Oxford Canal was shortened from ninety-one to seventy-seven and a half miles. Boats were allowed to travel by night as well as by day.

To attract traffic, canal companies dropped their tolls considerably. Even so, the profits on some waterways were so low that the companies were forced to sell up. Many railway companies bought up their rival canal companies. Some railway-owned canals were allowed to deteriorate until they were unusable, or their tolls were raised so much that they attracted no trade. Some canals were filled in and used as the route for railways.

How they lived

One of the main consequences of railway competition was that boatmen brought their families on to the boats to live and act as crew. Carriers had to economise by getting rid of their mate and boy, and selling the house ashore.

It sounds exciting to live on a boat, but it was a hard life, under very cramped conditions. The whole family helped. The parents usually steered and the older children walked with the horse or did the lock-wheeling, which meant walking or cycling ahead to get the locks ready. Winter months were particularly hard, when ropes were frozen and lock sides and boat decks were treacherous with ice.

Canal-boat people developed as a race apart, seldom leaving the canal side. Families gathered together for important occasions, like weddings and christenings. The parents sang and danced at canal-side inns and the boatmen played the melodeon and the mouth-organ.

Very few children could read or write as boats were seldom tied up in the same place for more than a short time and children were only able to snatch an occasional day's schooling.

The men folk did their fair share of poaching, with snare, dog and gun. They fished for eels using eel spears, which had long handles and flat, barbed prongs.

One of their favourite meals was the 'pail' dinner which consisted of turnips, rabbit, carrots, parsnips and potatoes, with a thick suet crust. Suet puddings were also very popular.

The narrow boat cabin

The boat cabin was about ten feet long, just under seven feet wide and five and a half feet high. Every inch of space was used economically to provide a comfortable home for the boatman and his family. Boat people were proud of their cabins and generally kept them attractive and spotlessly clean.

At the far end of the cabin was the main bed, with cupboards below and above it. The space it occupied was called the 'bunkhole'. On the right of the cabin was a single bed which served as sitting space in the day time. The door of the main food storage cupboard let down to make a table. On the left of the cabin was the coal-fired cooking range and above it, a brass drying rail.

The brass work around the stove and the chimney would always be highly polished. Boatwomen would crochet attractive curtains for the cabin and, round the cabin sides they would hang family photographs, horse brasses, and lace-edged plates, threaded with brightly coloured ribbons. They were proud of their huge Measham pottery teapots which were handed down from one generation to another. This was a brown, highly decorated style of pottery, often bearing inscriptions like 'Love at Home'.

The highly decorated water can and the mop lay on the cabin roof, with the mop pushed through the handle of the can, to keep it firm. Sometimes a horse's tail would hang from the rudder head, or 'Rams Head', which was decorated with intricate rope work.

Roses and castles

Nobody is certain of the origin of the 'Rose and Castle' design, which was used to decorate the inside and outside of the narrow boat cabin. Some people think that boat-people were of gypsy origin and that the painting was a survival of Romany art.

Another suggestion is that the castle represented the kilns of the Potteries, through which the boats passed and with which they traded. The pennant flying from one of the turrets represented the smoke, and the hills in the background were the heaps of waste material behind the kilns.

Possibly the castle was the boatman's idea of a dream home. Certainly, they were paintings of romantic castles, rather than medieval strongholds.

The roses may have been copies of dog-roses, growing around the doors of canal-side cottages, or on bushes along the canal bank.

There were examples of the 'Rose and Castle' design throughout almost the entire canal network, although there were local variations in style. Most boats were painted when they were in the boatyard for repair, and in prosperous times, a boat might be repainted every two years. There was some competition, especially between owner-boatmen, to possess the best decorated craft.

The boats were also decorated with good luck symbols, such as the ace-of-clubs design, hearts or anchors.

Clothing of the 'Cut'

Boat-people developed their own style of clothing. The men wore corduroy or moleskin trousers, striped collarless shirts, neckerchiefs and waistcoats. For 'best' they wore suits, usually black, and shirts which were often embroidered down the front. They were fond of leather brass-studded belts, but their best belts were made of canvas and were heavily embroidered in a multi-coloured criss-cross, or spider's web pattern. Their best braces were also multi-coloured.

The women wore ankle-length, striped skirts, long, wide aprons, blouses with 'leg of mutton' sleeves, shawls and bonnets. The bonnet had a brim stiffened with rows of corded quilting and frills or 'curtains', often in two layers, hanging over the shoulders. The 'curtains' were edged with crocheted lace. The bonnet strings were rarely worn tied.

The horse, an essential part of the team, was always well cared for. Towing ropes were threaded through brightly painted wooden bobbins which prevented chafing. Highly polished horse brasses hung from the leather martingale. Sometimes boatwomen would crochet ear protectors into which the horses' ears would be tucked to protect them from flies. Instead of nose feedbags, the canal horse had a metal bowl, always decorated with the traditional roses pattern, which was hung from the harness. Horses frequently needed new shoes, on average every two weeks, and there were blacksmith's shops at recognised stopping places up and down the canal.

Canal buildings

The canal line had to be maintained properly or traffic would soon be unable to move along it. Depots were set up where masons, carpenters, and shipwrights could work. At the depot at Ellesmere, on the Llangollen Canal, there is a boat dock, a lock gate shop and a blacksmith's shop.

In addition to the lock-keeper's cottages, there were houses for the wharfingers, who were the men in charge of the wharves, for the tunnel keepers and for the bridge-keepers who worked the swing bridges. Each canal had its own style of architecture. On the Stratford Canal there were barrel-roofed cottages built like tunnels, castellated brick 'roundhouses' on the Birmingham and Fazeley Canal and round tower lock-houses on the Thames and Severn Canal. Toll Offices, built for the clerks who collected tolls, were often octagonal in shape, with a central doorway, and side windows through which the clerk could see traffic approaching from either direction.

Many elegant pumping stations, which once housed the huge beam engines used to raise the water to high canal pounds, can still be seen. Warehouses were built, often standing on great arches over the canal, so that canal boats could be unloaded directly beneath the arches through trap doors built into the structure.

There were also many public houses, built near towns and villages, to provide refreshment for boatmen and passengers. At frequent intervals, too, there were stables, sometimes capable of holding a dozen or more animals.

Ship canals in Britain

One reason for constructing a Ship Canal could be to avoid a long, or hazardous sea journey. The Caledonian Canal, linking the North Sea to the Atlantic, saved a long voyage round the north coast of Scotland. Another Scottish Ship Canal, the Crinan, was intended to save the eighty-five mile journey round the Kintyre Peninsula.

A Ship Canal might also be constructed to link a town to the sea, or to bypass a difficult or dangerous river. Efforts were made, as early as 1563, to dig a canal to Exeter so that the woollen goods produced in the city could be easily exported. Gloucester became a busy port after the construction of the Gloucester and Berkeley Ship Canal which was built to avoid a treacherous part of the River Severn.

These Ship Canals are small, however, compared with the mighty Manchester Ship Canal, which was opened by Queen Victoria in 1894. The line of the canal was planned to pass beneath James Brindley's Barton Aqueduct, which carried the Bridgewater Canal over the River Irwell. The Aqueduct was removed and a swing aqueduct erected, which can be opened to allow large ships to pass. The biggest lock on the Canal is six hundred feet long and eighty feet wide and ships of twelve thousand tons can navigate to Manchester's inland port. The Canal has brought such prosperity that Manchester is now the third most important port in the country, and handles over five thousand ships each year.